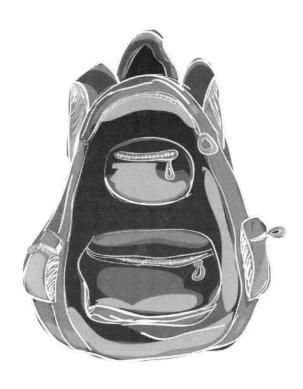

This Travel Journal Belongs To:

_____
_____
_____

 # A Cool Thing About Today

My Trip To:

Today's Date: _____

Location: _____

Weather: ☀   ☁   🌧   🌨

This Day Was:
☐ Awesome ☐ Great ☐ Fun ☐ Okay

I spent the day with:
_____
_____
_____

The best part of the day was:
_____
_____
_____

The yummiest food I ate today was:
_____
_____

One interesting thing I learned today was:
_____
_____

Today's Favorite Memory

_____
_____
_____
_____
_____

A Cool Thing About Today

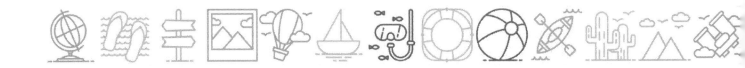

My Trip To:

Today's Date: _____

Location: _____

Weather: *This Day Was:*
☐ Awesome ☐ Great ☐ Fun ☐ Okay

I spent the day with:
_____
_____
_____

The best part of the day was:
_____
_____
_____

The yummiest food I ate today was:
_____
_____

One interesting thing I learned today was:
_____
_____

Today's Favorite Memory
_____
_____
_____
_____
_____

 # A Cool Thing About Today

My Trip To:

Today's Date: _____

Location: _____

Weather: ☀ ☁ 🌧 🌨

This Day Was:
☐ Awesome ☐ Great ☐ Fun ☐ Okay

I spent the day with:
_____
_____
_____

The best part of the day was:
_____
_____
_____

The yummiest food I ate today was:
_____
_____

One interesting thing I learned today was:
_____
_____

Today's Favorite Memory
_____
_____
_____
_____
_____

 # A Cool Thing About Today

My Trip To:

Today's Date: _____

Location: _____

Weather: ☀ ☁ ☂ ❄

This Day Was:
☐ Awesome ☐ Great ☐ Fun ☐ Okay

I spent the day with:
_____
_____
_____

The best part of the day was:
_____
_____
_____

The yummiest food I ate today was:
_____
_____

One interesting thing I learned today was:
_____
_____

Today's Favorite Memory

_____
_____
_____
_____
_____

 # A Cool Thing About Today

My Trip To:

Today's Date: _____

Location: _____

Weather: ☀ ☁ ☂ ❄

This Day Was:
☐ Awesome ☐ Great ☐ Fun ☐ Okay

I spent the day with:
_____
_____
_____

The best part of the day was:
_____
_____
_____

The yummiest food I ate today was:
_____
_____

One interesting thing I learned today was:
_____
_____

Today's Favorite Memory
_____
_____
_____
_____
_____

 # A Cool Thing About Today

My Trip To:

Today's Date: _____

Location: _____

Weather: ☀ ☁ 🌧 🌨

This Day Was:
☐ Awesome ☐ Great ☐ Fun ☐ Okay

I spent the day with:
_____
_____
_____

The best part of the day was:
_____
_____
_____

The yummiest food I ate today was:
_____
_____

One interesting thing I learned today was:
_____
_____

Today's Favorite Memory
_____
_____
_____
_____
_____

 # A Cool Thing About Today

My Trip To:

Today's Date: _____

Location: _____

Weather: *This Day Was:*
☐ Awesome ☐ Great ☐ Fun ☐ Okay

I spent the day with:
_____
_____
_____

The best part of the day was:
_____
_____
_____

The yummiest food I ate today was:
_____
_____

One interesting thing I learned today was:
_____
_____

Today's Favorite Memory
_____
_____
_____
_____
_____

 # A Cool Thing About Today

My Trip To:

Today's Date: _____

Location: _____

Weather: *This Day Was:*
☐ Awesome ☐ Great ☐ Fun ☐ Okay

I spent the day with:
_____
_____
_____

The best part of the day was:
_____
_____
_____

The yummiest food I ate today was:
_____
_____

One interesting thing I learned today was:
_____
_____

Today's Favorite Memory

_____
_____
_____
_____
_____

 # A Cool Thing About Today

My Trip To:

Today's Date: _____

Location: _____

Weather: ☀ ☁ 🌧 🌨

This Day Was:
☐ Awesome ☐ Great ☐ Fun ☐ Okay

I spent the day with:
_____
_____
_____

The best part of the day was:
_____
_____
_____

The yummiest food I ate today was:
_____
_____

One interesting thing I learned today was:
_____
_____

Today's Favorite Memory
_____
_____
_____
_____
_____

 # A Cool Thing About Today

My Trip To:

Today's Date: _____

Location: _____

Weather: ☀   ☁   🌧   🌨

This Day Was:
☐ Awesome   ☐ Great   ☐ Fun   ☐ Okay

I spent the day with:
_____
_____
_____

The best part of the day was:
_____
_____
_____

The yummiest food I ate today was:
_____
_____

One interesting thing I learned today was:
_____
_____

Today's Favorite Memory
_____
_____
_____
_____
_____

 # A Cool Thing About Today

My Trip To:

Today's Date: _____

Location: _____

Weather: ☀ ☁ 🌧 🌨

This Day Was:
☐ Awesome ☐ Great ☐ Fun ☐ Okay

I spent the day with:
_____
_____
_____

The best part of the day was:
_____
_____
_____

The yummiest food I ate today was:
_____
_____

One interesting thing I learned today was:
_____
_____

Today's Favorite Memory
_____
_____
_____
_____
_____

 # A Cool Thing About Today

My Trip To:

Today's Date: _____

Location: _____

Weather: ☀ ☁ 🌧 🌨

This Day Was:
☐ Awesome ☐ Great ☐ Fun ☐ Okay

I spent the day with:
_____
_____
_____

The best part of the day was:
_____
_____
_____

The yummiest food I ate today was:
_____
_____

One interesting thing I learned today was:
_____
_____

Today's Favorite Memory
_____
_____
_____
_____
_____

 # A Cool Thing About Today

My Trip To:

Today's Date: _____

Location: _____

Weather: ☀️ ☁️ 🌧️ ❄️

This Day Was:
☐ Awesome ☐ Great ☐ Fun ☐ Okay

I spent the day with:
_____
_____
_____

The best part of the day was:
_____
_____
_____

The yummiest food I ate today was:
_____
_____

One interesting thing I learned today was:
_____
_____

Today's Favorite Memory

_____
_____
_____
_____
_____

A Cool Thing About Today

My Trip To:

Today's Date: _____

Location: _____

Weather: ☀ ☁ 🌧 🌨

This Day Was:
☐ Awesome ☐ Great ☐ Fun ☐ Okay

I spent the day with:
_____
_____
_____

The best part of the day was:
_____
_____
_____

The yummiest food I ate today was:
_____
_____

One interesting thing I learned today was:
_____
_____

Today's Favorite Memory

_____
_____
_____
_____
_____

# A Cool Thing About Today

My Trip To:

Today's Date: _____

Location: _____

Weather: ☀ ☁ 🌧 ❄   *This Day Was:*
☐ Awesome ☐ Great ☐ Fun ☐ Okay

I spent the day with:
_____
_____
_____

The best part of the day was:
_____
_____
_____

The yummiest food I ate today was:
_____
_____

One interesting thing I learned today was:
_____
_____

Today's Favorite Memory
_____
_____
_____
_____
_____

 # A Cool Thing About Today

My Trip To:

Today's Date: _____

Location: _____

Weather: ☀ ☁ 🌧 🌨   *This Day Was:* ☐ Awesome ☐ Great ☐ Fun ☐ Okay

I spent the day with:
_____
_____
_____

The best part of the day was:
_____
_____
_____

The yummiest food I ate today was:
_____
_____

One interesting thing I learned today was:
_____
_____

Today's Favorite Memory

_____
_____
_____
_____
_____

 # A Cool Thing About Today

My Trip To:

Today's Date: _____

Location: _____

Weather: ☀ ☁ 🌧 🌨

This Day Was:
☐ Awesome ☐ Great ☐ Fun ☐ Okay

I spent the day with:
_____
_____
_____

The best part of the day was:
_____
_____
_____

The yummiest food I ate today was:
_____
_____

One interesting thing I learned today was:
_____
_____

Today's Favorite Memory

_____
_____
_____
_____
_____

 # A Cool Thing About Today

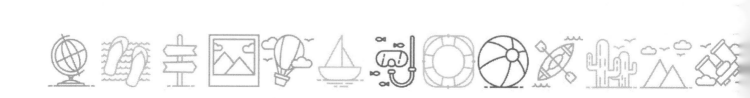

My Trip To:

Today's Date: _____

Location: _____

Weather: ☀ ☁ 🌧 ❄

This Day Was:
☐ Awesome ☐ Great ☐ Fun ☐ Okay

I spent the day with:
_____
_____
_____

The best part of the day was:
_____
_____
_____

The yummiest food I ate today was:
_____
_____

One interesting thing I learned today was:
_____
_____

Today's Favorite Memory
_____
_____
_____
_____
_____
_____

 # A Cool Thing About Today

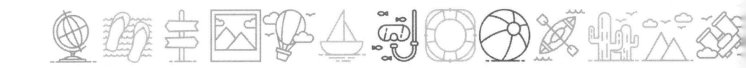

My Trip To:

Today's Date: _____

Location: _____

Weather: ☀ ☁ 🌧 🌨   ┌─── *This Day Was:* ───┐
                     ☐ Awesome ☐ Great ☐ Fun ☐ Okay

I spent the day with:
_____
_____
_____

The best part of the day was:
_____
_____
_____

The yummiest food I ate today was:
_____
_____

One interesting thing I learned today was:
_____
_____

Today's Favorite Memory
_____
_____
_____
_____
_____

 # A Cool Thing About Today

My Trip To:

Today's Date: _____

Location: _____

Weather: ☀ ☁ 🌧 ❄   *This Day Was:* ☐ Awesome ☐ Great ☐ Fun ☐ Okay

I spent the day with:
_____
_____
_____

The best part of the day was:
_____
_____
_____

The yummiest food I ate today was:
_____
_____

One interesting thing I learned today was:
_____
_____

Today's Favorite Memory
_____
_____
_____
_____
_____

 # A Cool Thing About Today

My Trip To:

Today's Date: _____

Location: _____

Weather: ☀ ☁ 🌧 🌨

This Day Was:
☐ Awesome ☐ Great ☐ Fun ☐ Okay

I spent the day with:
_____
_____
_____

The best part of the day was:
_____
_____
_____

The yummiest food I ate today was:
_____
_____

One interesting thing I learned today was:
_____
_____

Today's Favorite Memory
_____
_____
_____
_____
_____

A Cool Thing About Today

My Trip To:

Today's Date: _____

Location: _____

Weather: ☀ ☁ 🌧 🌨

This Day Was:
☐ Awesome   ☐ Great   ☐ Fun   ☐ Okay

I spent the day with:
_____
_____
_____

The best part of the day was:
_____
_____
_____

The yummiest food I ate today was:
_____
_____

One interesting thing I learned today was:
_____
_____

Today's Favorite Memory
_____
_____
_____
_____
_____

 # A Cool Thing About Today

My Trip To:

Today's Date: _____

Location: _____

Weather: *This Day Was:*
☐ Awesome ☐ Great ☐ Fun ☐ Okay

I spent the day with:
_____
_____
_____

The best part of the day was:
_____
_____
_____

The yummiest food I ate today was:
_____
_____

One interesting thing I learned today was:
_____
_____

Today's Favorite Memory

_____
_____
_____
_____
_____

 # A Cool Thing About Today

My Trip To:

Today's Date: _____

Location: _____

Weather: ☀   ☁   🌧   🌨

This Day Was:
☐ Awesome ☐ Great ☐ Fun ☐ Okay

I spent the day with:
_____
_____
_____

The best part of the day was:
_____
_____
_____

The yummiest food I ate today was:
_____
_____

One interesting thing I learned today was:
_____
_____

Today's Favorite Memory
_____
_____
_____
_____
_____

 # A Cool Thing About Today

My Trip To:

Today's Date: _____

Location: _____

Weather: ☀ ☁ ☂ ❄

This Day Was:
☐ Awesome ☐ Great ☐ Fun ☐ Okay

I spent the day with:
_____
_____
_____

The best part of the day was:
_____
_____
_____

The yummiest food I ate today was:
_____
_____

One interesting thing I learned today was:
_____
_____

Today's Favorite Memory
_____
_____
_____
_____
_____

 # A Cool Thing About Today

My Trip To:

Today's Date: _____

Location: _____

Weather: ☀ ☁ ⛈ ❄

This Day Was:
☐ Awesome ☐ Great ☐ Fun ☐ Okay

I spent the day with:
_____
_____
_____

The best part of the day was:
_____
_____
_____

The yummiest food I ate today was:
_____
_____

One interesting thing I learned today was:
_____
_____

Today's Favorite Memory
_____
_____
_____
_____
_____

 # A Cool Thing About Today

My Trip To:

Today's Date: _____

Location: _____

Weather: ☀ ☁ 🌧 ❄

This Day Was:
☐ Awesome ☐ Great ☐ Fun ☐ Okay

I spent the day with:
_____
_____
_____

The best part of the day was:
_____
_____
_____

The yummiest food I ate today was:
_____
_____

One interesting thing I learned today was:
_____
_____

Today's Favorite Memory
_____
_____
_____
_____
_____
_____

 # A Cool Thing About Today

My Trip To:

Today's Date: _____

Location: _____

Weather: ☀ ☁ 🌧 ❄   *This Day Was:* ☐ Awesome ☐ Great ☐ Fun ☐ Okay

I spent the day with:
_____
_____
_____

The best part of the day was:
_____
_____
_____

The yummiest food I ate today was:
_____
_____

One interesting thing I learned today was:
_____
_____

Today's Favorite Memory
_____
_____
_____
_____
_____

A Cool Thing About Today

My Trip To:

Today's Date: _____

Location: _____

Weather: ☀ ☁ 🌧 ❄   *This Day Was:* ☐ Awesome ☐ Great ☐ Fun ☐ Okay

I spent the day with:
_____
_____
_____

The best part of the day was:
_____
_____
_____

The yummiest food I ate today was:
_____
_____

One interesting thing I learned today was:
_____
_____

Today's Favorite Memory
_____
_____
_____
_____
_____

 # A Cool Thing About Today

My Trip To:

Today's Date: _____

Location: _____

Weather: ☀   ☁   🌧   🌨

This Day Was:
☐ Awesome   ☐ Great   ☐ Fun   ☐ Okay

I spent the day with:
_____
_____
_____

The best part of the day was:
_____
_____
_____

The yummiest food I ate today was:
_____
_____

One interesting thing I learned today was:
_____
_____

Today's Favorite Memory
_____
_____
_____
_____
_____
_____

 # A Cool Thing About Today

My Trip To:

Today's Date: _____

Location: _____

Weather: ☀ ☁ 🌧 🌨

This Day Was:
☐ Awesome ☐ Great ☐ Fun ☐ Okay

I spent the day with:
_____
_____
_____

The best part of the day was:
_____
_____
_____

The yummiest food I ate today was:
_____
_____

One interesting thing I learned today was:
_____
_____

Today's Favorite Memory

_____
_____
_____
_____
_____

 # A Cool Thing About Today

My Trip To:

Today's Date: _____

Location: _____

Weather: ☀ ☁ 🌧 🌨

This Day Was:
☐ Awesome ☐ Great ☐ Fun ☐ Okay

I spent the day with:
_____
_____
_____

The best part of the day was:
_____
_____
_____

The yummiest food I ate today was:
_____
_____

One interesting thing I learned today was:
_____
_____

Today's Favorite Memory

_____
_____
_____
_____
_____

 # A Cool Thing About Today

My Trip To:

Today's Date: _____

Location: _____

Weather: ☀ ☁ 🌧 🌨

This Day Was:
☐ Awesome ☐ Great ☐ Fun ☐ Okay

I spent the day with:
_____
_____
_____

The best part of the day was:
_____
_____
_____

The yummiest food I ate today was:
_____
_____

One interesting thing I learned today was:
_____
_____

Today's Favorite Memory
_____
_____
_____
_____
_____
_____

 # A Cool Thing About Today

My Trip To:

Today's Date: _____

Location: _____

Weather: ☀ ☁ 🌧 🌨

This Day Was:
☐ Awesome ☐ Great ☐ Fun ☐ Okay

I spent the day with:
_____
_____
_____

The best part of the day was:
_____
_____
_____

The yummiest food I ate today was:
_____
_____

One interesting thing I learned today was:
_____
_____

Today's Favorite Memory
_____
_____
_____
_____
_____

 # A Cool Thing About Today

My Trip To:

Today's Date: _____

Location: _____

Weather: ☀ ☁ 🌧 🌨

This Day Was:
☐ Awesome ☐ Great ☐ Fun ☐ Okay

I spent the day with:
_____
_____
_____

The best part of the day was:
_____
_____
_____

The yummiest food I ate today was:
_____
_____

One interesting thing I learned today was:
_____
_____

Today's Favorite Memory
_____
_____
_____
_____
_____

 # A Cool Thing About Today

My Trip To:

Today's Date: _____

Location: _____

Weather: ☀ ☁ 🌧 🌨   *This Day Was:* ☐ Awesome ☐ Great ☐ Fun ☐ Okay

I spent the day with:

_____
_____
_____

The best part of the day was:

_____
_____
_____

The yummiest food I ate today was:

_____
_____

One interesting thing I learned today was:

_____
_____

Today's Favorite Memory

_____
_____
_____
_____
_____

 # A Cool Thing About Today

My Trip To:

Today's Date: _____

Location: _____

Weather: ☀   ☁   🌧   ❄

This Day Was:
☐ Awesome ☐ Great ☐ Fun ☐ Okay

I spent the day with:
_____
_____
_____

The best part of the day was:
_____
_____
_____

The yummiest food I ate today was:
_____
_____

One interesting thing I learned today was:
_____
_____

Today's Favorite Memory

_____
_____
_____
_____
_____

 # A Cool Thing About Today

My Trip To:

Today's Date: _____

Location: _____

Weather: ☀ ☁ 🌧 ❄

This Day Was:
☐ Awesome ☐ Great ☐ Fun ☐ Okay

I spent the day with:
_____
_____
_____

The best part of the day was:
_____
_____
_____

The yummiest food I ate today was:
_____
_____

One interesting thing I learned today was:
_____
_____

Today's Favorite Memory
_____
_____
_____
_____
_____

 # A Cool Thing About Today

My Trip To:

Today's Date: _____

Location: _____

Weather: ☀   ☁   🌧   🌨

This Day Was:
☐ Awesome ☐ Great ☐ Fun ☐ Okay

I spent the day with:
_____
_____
_____

The best part of the day was:
_____
_____
_____

The yummiest food I ate today was:
_____
_____

One interesting thing I learned today was:
_____
_____

Today's Favorite Memory
_____
_____
_____
_____
_____
_____

 # A Cool Thing About Today

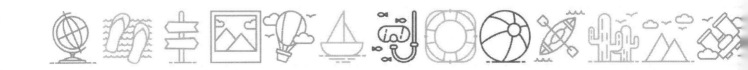

My Trip To:

Today's Date: _____

Location: _____

Weather: ☀ ☁ 🌧 🌨

This Day Was:
☐ Awesome   ☐ Great   ☐ Fun   ☐ Okay

I spent the day with:
_____
_____
_____

The best part of the day was:
_____
_____
_____

The yummiest food I ate today was:
_____
_____

One interesting thing I learned today was:
_____
_____

Today's Favorite Memory
_____
_____
_____
_____
_____

 # A Cool Thing About Today

My Trip To:

Today's Date: _____

Location: _____

Weather: ☀ ☁ 🌧 ❄

This Day Was:
☐ Awesome ☐ Great ☐ Fun ☐ Okay

I spent the day with:
_____
_____
_____

The best part of the day was:
_____
_____
_____

The yummiest food I ate today was:
_____
_____

One interesting thing I learned today was:
_____
_____

Today's Favorite Memory
_____
_____
_____
_____
_____

 # A Cool Thing About Today

My Trip To:

Today's Date: _____

Location: _____

Weather:

This Day Was:
☐ Awesome ☐ Great ☐ Fun ☐ Okay

I spent the day with:
_____
_____
_____

The best part of the day was:
_____
_____
_____

The yummiest food I ate today was:
_____
_____

One interesting thing I learned today was:
_____
_____

Today's Favorite Memory
_____
_____
_____
_____
_____

 # A Cool Thing About Today

My Trip To:

Today's Date: _____

Location: _____

Weather: ☀ ☁ 🌧 ❄

This Day Was:
☐ Awesome ☐ Great ☐ Fun ☐ Okay

I spent the day with:
_____
_____
_____

The best part of the day was:
_____
_____
_____

The yummiest food I ate today was:
_____
_____

One interesting thing I learned today was:
_____
_____
_____

Today's Favorite Memory
_____
_____
_____
_____
_____

 # A Cool Thing About Today

My Trip To:

Today's Date: _____

Location: _____

Weather: ☀ ☁ ☔ ❄

This Day Was:
☐ Awesome ☐ Great ☐ Fun ☐ Okay

I spent the day with:
_____
_____
_____

The best part of the day was:
_____
_____
_____

The yummiest food I ate today was:
_____
_____

One interesting thing I learned today was:
_____
_____

Today's Favorite Memory
_____
_____
_____
_____
_____

 # A Cool Thing About Today

My Trip To:

Today's Date: _____

Location: _____

Weather: ☀ ☁ 🌧 🌨

This Day Was:
☐ Awesome ☐ Great ☐ Fun ☐ Okay

I spent the day with:
_____
_____
_____

The best part of the day was:
_____
_____
_____

The yummiest food I ate today was:
_____
_____

One interesting thing I learned today was:
_____
_____

Today's Favorite Memory
_____
_____
_____
_____
_____

 # A Cool Thing About Today

My Trip To:

Today's Date: _____

Location: _____

Weather: ☀ ☁ ☔ ❄

This Day Was:
☐ Awesome ☐ Great ☐ Fun ☐ Okay

I spent the day with:
_____
_____
_____

The best part of the day was:
_____
_____
_____

The yummiest food I ate today was:
_____
_____

One interesting thing I learned today was:
_____
_____

Today's Favorite Memory
_____
_____
_____
_____
_____

 # A Cool Thing About Today

My Trip To:

Today's Date: _____

Location: _____

Weather: ☀   ☁   🌧   ❄

This Day Was:
☐ Awesome   ☐ Great   ☐ Fun   ☐ Okay

I spent the day with:
_____
_____
_____

The best part of the day was:
_____
_____
_____

The yummiest food I ate today was:
_____
_____

One interesting thing I learned today was:
_____
_____

Today's Favorite Memory
_____
_____
_____
_____
_____

 # A Cool Thing About Today

My Trip To:

Today's Date: _____

Location: _____

Weather: ☀ ☁ 🌧 🌨

This Day Was:
☐ Awesome ☐ Great ☐ Fun ☐ Okay

I spent the day with:
_____
_____
_____

The best part of the day was:
_____
_____
_____

The yummiest food I ate today was:
_____
_____

One interesting thing I learned today was:
_____
_____

Today's Favorite Memory

_____
_____
_____
_____
_____
_____

 # A Cool Thing About Today

My Trip To:

Today's Date: _____

Location: _____

Weather:

This Day Was:
☐ Awesome ☐ Great ☐ Fun ☐ Okay

I spent the day with:
_____
_____
_____

The best part of the day was:
_____
_____
_____

The yummiest food I ate today was:
_____
_____

One interesting thing I learned today was:
_____
_____

Today's Favorite Memory
_____
_____
_____
_____
_____

 # A Cool Thing About Today

My Trip To:

Today's Date: _____

Location: _____

Weather: ☀ ☁ ⛈ ❄

This Day Was:
☐ Awesome ☐ Great ☐ Fun ☐ Okay

I spent the day with:
_____
_____
_____

The best part of the day was:
_____
_____
_____

The yummiest food I ate today was:
_____
_____

One interesting thing I learned today was:
_____
_____

Today's Favorite Memory
_____
_____
_____
_____
_____
_____

 # A Cool Thing About Today

My Trip To:

Today's Date: _____

Location: _____

Weather: ☀   ☁   🌧   ❄

This Day Was:
☐ Awesome ☐ Great ☐ Fun ☐ Okay

I spent the day with:
_____
_____
_____

The best part of the day was:
_____
_____
_____

The yummiest food I ate today was:
_____
_____

One interesting thing I learned today was:
_____
_____

Today's Favorite Memory
_____
_____
_____
_____
_____

 # A Cool Thing About Today

My Trip To:

Today's Date: _____

Location: _____

Weather:

This Day Was:
☐ Awesome ☐ Great ☐ Fun ☐ Okay

I spent the day with:
_____
_____
_____

The best part of the day was:
_____
_____
_____

The yummiest food I ate today was:
_____
_____

One interesting thing I learned today was:
_____
_____

Today's Favorite Memory
_____
_____
_____
_____
_____

 # A Cool Thing About Today

My Trip To:

Today's Date: _____

Location: _____

Weather: ☀ ☁ ☂ ❄

This Day Was:
☐ Awesome ☐ Great ☐ Fun ☐ Okay

I spent the day with:
_____
_____
_____

The best part of the day was:
_____
_____
_____

The yummiest food I ate today was:
_____
_____

One interesting thing I learned today was:
_____
_____

Today's Favorite Memory

_____
_____
_____
_____
_____

 # A Cool Thing About Today

My Trip To:

Today's Date: _____

Location: _____

Weather: ☀   ☁   🌧   🌨

This Day Was:
☐ Awesome ☐ Great ☐ Fun ☐ Okay

I spent the day with:
_____
_____
_____

The best part of the day was:
_____
_____
_____

The yummiest food I ate today was:
_____
_____

One interesting thing I learned today was:
_____
_____

Today's Favorite Memory
_____
_____
_____
_____
_____

Made in United States
Orlando, FL
19 May 2022